W9-CLN-879

RIGHT NEW BIOLOGY

DATE DUE

Demco, Inc. 38-293

DEC 0 7 2009

RIGHT NEW BIOLOGY

kathryn l. pringle

Factory School, 2009
Queens, New York

RIGHT NEW BIOLOGY
by kathryn l. pringle

Heretical Texts
Volume 4, Number 2

Factory School
Queens, NY, 2009

ISBN (paperback): 978-1-60001-057-6
ISBN (hardcover): 978-1-60001-058-3

Cover art by Danielle Lawrence, © 2008

Many thanks to the editors of the following journals in which excerpts from/versions of this poem have previously appeared: *Alice Blue, Dusie, effing magazine, foursquare, RIFE*, and *string of small machines*.

My deep gratitude goes to CAConrad for his support of this manuscript, and Andrea Rexilius for sharing her careful, enlightened reading with me during the early drafts. For years of care and poetic support above and beyond, I would like to thank Magdalena Zurawski. Big thank yous go to Elise Ficarra, Chris Vitiello, Erin Wilson, Jessica Smith, Dianne Timblin, Jamie Lewis, Guillermo Parra, Ken Rumble, Kate Colby, Kate Schapira, Kate Greenstreet, Des Peterson, Colleen Lennon, and Judith Goldman, for friendship and general psychology. And thank you, Patrice Jleaun, for over twenty years of asking the hard questions—knowing the answers—and patiently waiting for me to know them, too.

This book could not have been written without the influence of many Presidents of the United States of America and Sigmund Freud.

Factory School is a learning and production collective engaged in action research, multiple-media arts, publishing, and community service.

For more information, please visit factoryschool.org

for US

RIGHT NEW BIOLOGY

i's laughing at what's ems in the GROUP
but i can't lick the interest
yes i's drunk, but i can build
[no shrank when a cannot is spoken

                        we barks and shits
when the VERSE opens

character heads west
                two full – nothing happens

not a garden, not an analyzed erotic
a sparse production RIGHT
            having us //
                    (inside the CONFLICT
                    (erased citizen

these outright
individuals

even so little
are laughing ORGANS

at the nothing happens
kultur gangster, kultur warden
offer their eyes that not

sum of   individual
in them
was another

diseased
ORDINANCE
cast wending leaden lung of
W–.

a shining ditch
against
bitter form
a good tale a stout beer and one question
WE ones is not remainder, NATURE its
LUNG of spirit – the MASS WILL
is only shits problems

all's SINGING for the ordained
refrigerator humming
a call to ARMS
and FUR
the SUPERMARKET establishment
the ENGINEER of prozac
: a heist
of character

leaving elicits

SELF o, foul there
breaking tacit physiology
oceans of words flanked
by yet anOTHER

      i is self AMERIKAND
            woe these not
      angels a friend to
      not refuse a tree

when night is unassisted trench
von vielen anderen bedauerte woman
[in TEXT]

this, the nervous order of the day in two forms
one exhaustion
two sympathetic
three dialogic
crossroad # 309.15A: ENTRANCE
contemporary

CRESCENDO

begin here

[pretense]

RED and WHITE of the radio
tower – we is prime untenable
     space. consequence of entering
set: purple mountained.   AMERIKA
                    is
              uniformed and
              "bricks
      ideal locomotive – can be
      organized as well as dis
      evidenced behind text
      in the atoms
      of the white

      surface. we inhales, we

      placed in parts. in a stadium
structure of capitalist intent, no
such apparatus riding
     only prime density –

diesel:

fused fair // reign not // twice
drunk from the designs made by (love)
the tree or the work, or
a tree and a work
                 is not daring – does not befriend

out of them   y.1938 specifically 1930

this unbecoming
culture: can of
EINER RED and PEOPLE, all night words

{design}   apparent becomes fundamental
in armed intervention
          manacled veins

augment distended rampant fertilization uniformed
WESTERN LICHEN. THE FUNDAMENTAL.

WE is a working number that neuters
having had grief bare. set speaker
thought sexual with a fast story o
f it – THE OBJECT –

diesel burns. the building a dove
offers her body   a name
while sadistic.   outer beam
             rift between
                  falling

on land

without resentment shining animal
stricken // libido driven – WE having
had grief – AND RIGHT NEW
BIOLOGY
            this

-ALITY now a person aching

having spectacle, all so
(the second human lights us

who dead end cadence the ver-

be lieved most in day, come bound such fairer
a fill hedge see lean is told all into lect-
end how TRANSPARANCY

stave core cistern

flee und goes half won AM, ONE pretty ition,
SEX is ever many have it

work of spectacle
wants the idle less sent s o (u)s
a cracker OPERAtion in ovation

(to inherit
      acreage: etched fine
      absorbed diffuse color

                  s

            i is not fall
            in flat squares, i is
                    supine extended
            against the more

          passing away
          fade traced
          beneath the place–
                  bereft dissolve)

with tact so peak the opus
misery vital of made is ego proper [the]
licking of saving [the] by caused is sadness
FARM is vocation // is a perhaps
anything // advocate // DO

o we knows skeptic, is is

[the which] IMMORTALITY
            UNTOWARD elegy filch window

the LUNGS, asthmatic gutters, press in
lanky: JUST

EMPIRE of VALUES
        und raising traditions the risers
before we allegianced
absolved the FoUNDING
          —a tendered organ
             the nothing happens
all RED and PRE
recorded tapes   a damp burning out of PALMS
and the city a HILL // upon
we's all JUST
in INSTITUTIONal
          i'zed canvassed POLLED a
conCENSUS of one
          PRINCIPLEd INTEREST

//

(ENDpunkers enter the understanding

of the reading

not the actual
nor the inactual

performance:

THEY bringing how flammable
in train
sickly
is only

the ground. the pedestrian

           all the pretty
                softened
          preamble
          striking key, the
                  means
         a
   hammer

to spin, to spin
wound form sailing
a phonograph:

        -------*)

aftersight outfitted in blindness about the first hung shoulders in
ideal stereo – the INDIVIDUAL going yonder over the people //
encumbrance undercover // a return a stark endsight – an urgent
denial question:: dark analytical others // not light, the

leaving over all

and the living strive in this way

that sincere shot unintended is the much to question

arrives by
air.
current evolutions
demeanor the atmosphere
in tenor

pose for affection
climbing
along the torso feel
muscle beneath skin

the sky; a
firmament

mental acuity beguiles
repetition, cries into
nape,
or a tune
we is

tails. says away as one in white melodic
calls them the schema I has an angry genome
how we or us
in which correct EMPIRE return
how such inscripted EGO

a MANUSCRIPT W/ MANY TIGHTLY WORKED PHRASES

how kind a sea is here
for cited WAR
      apparitions mention funeral
      return the CAPITAL is here
      closed by salt against:
                      CRAFT
dragging behind eight lips
is a late fascicle – UNrelievable END NOMMEN
lengthens a SELFhood by lesions this, the GENESIS
Lot's wife will survive. daughters will have to
fuck him in other ways.

this.
the nervous order of the day.
in two forms.
one. exhaustion.
two. sympathetic.
three. dialogic.

crossroad #310.15A: ENTRANCE

        stones dog the heart
        that unbellowing
        stammered
        canal

of WE, this daily levees – distance.

weighted not in swimming across that ocean
AUGHT when each PRAY and ILLUSION
handedness time is
befriending the instance

from them we
what we knows
PSYCHE

HERE, as an answer, WHERE, as an
arbitrary rending

[that she was a NUN]

is only twice what we knows first

of long peace | war, the HISTORY says
of our NERVOUS SYSTEMS, the guests

building sin enfold the verging:
organs and their ornamental places

WAR among escalation is a desirous term.

[pretense]

the underside along the PERIPHERY our selenium
there are infused being unwise: it is a quality we
                              hears EVEN so
in it we all goes how I and FORESIGHT go
a tight KNOWING of facts   found empirical this
function here   out of TONGUE   [the waterfalls
where all langering furls from endorphins to WAR
RIGHT THINKING ARMS   adequate
what is to carry we FOrward? INHALE.
does not give
                   in such a way buys
commodity. CENSURE INSTRINSIC
features allow tobacco peace – INFILTRATE
UPwards men women, whom legitimate
diction first writer your errand is large
foreshadow's done. OR whom the tight
wisdom asks of dares   abwaltzing never
                              that glutton

i is self AMERI
un der e quell d
of not.

when we is BEREFT of place
we upENDS places
               try, too, to be – so hard
sought SUB
-structure is bottom
is eighty percent of not
just this of not
JUST this politik
body drawn geographic
of not just. of not, just

      a lone VERNACULAR
      squint. through ANGST

      for them. that were
      eyes. elder phylo leave
      lust dim. the ACADEMY
      of remaindering dour.

      but w/ LANGUAGE

phrasing, that engine
is it one. we wills
reality: three stark
three answers. integrity
existence & method a
drunken REALISTIK sign

with LANGUAGE

in the pipes a high whine
through the CENTRAL PASSAGE
UNDERout. of street furor. through
the SOLUTION's BAILing alone
wise. in (like mind) or kind genetics

hearing ruined how it before
then was a fetish of
MERE ACRES

we hasn't the HEARING
       that day's switch and ill FERVENT
       wish has this the self halting
       question the spirit that has shined
when betoning the all's PERVERSion
       (that REALITY SPAKES

it speaketh a gentle (twice broken neurotik

the biPARTISANs glimmer
       a twinkle

i's likens the symptoms of -ses
as FUNKTION. as
indulgence. as all out WATERs OCEANs

as incremental distribution
instrumental now under blunt signs
cross backwords
falling over & AUCTIONed

at the bottom 80—so it is DAMMING
        of the 100.
        of the whole DAMN
that place that we is
bereft of. ONE
be placeless and not
one   . we is   a single threat

all hung // at a slant.

ROLL underworn sullen whom ripe for task
is seeking – EINER gelatin craft unseen
FALL and ACHE: DICTATOR
head bulldozing a gear shifting   a had
this ONE dares under
knowing we naught

and of THEM twice drunken dear grounds
these here unknowing hidden have here in
sincere language. A SHAFT GIVEN SWAY. we has
us here them next moss we takes on waiting
answers close getting this, the order of the day

and the living strive in this way

that sincere shot
is the much to question

enters i's the over-i's the
one thought on this folding

remembers now the PLEA

FREE eye is landing on
MONOPOLY

the GREEN in thine of I has it
broader terms: given / taken
the DREAM brings another
dungeon:
gender: swing
gender

there are only ever three: drei
functions of insult:

early symbolic bedtime
hazing I morning I a

sapling
empire disguised then
with INHALE makes dead is counter
correctwise we goes our
duty of three sleeping the light

quite: *sehr haüfig Eindrücke*

we forages und clears
ACTIVisms gives mettle
an aching PRAXIS
this patriotISM

we knows WAR not a financial apron
change clamors to cement
floor we knows
interrogation
s spiked w/ tepid

water .

three .

     inches .

        deep .

a mask a mask
we KNOWS

the answers, this

EINER RED and PEOPLE, all night words

open SKY like INQUISITION

mention KULTUR thus hell and objective
level through subjective habits WE
lassens against a mute SUM
o, happy SITUATIONists
               EMPIRE.

we straw characters of dreams, we
knows spontaneity   INTERCOURSE
we knows the POSITION OF TRAUMA

three salvagers part the inhibition
tendons has lock// unsure: theory
speak faster
spacious reproducer

time in vocabulary : actuary

ich schriebe natur:
                    TRAUMENSTELLUNG

we knows eggs crash from wearing

INHALE.

a man, for example divine, is undereye so taken this art of middle
long what is seen – permitted / that's just TORN / broken muscle
AND RIGHT NEW BIOLOGY
the study flees BEING also all the all knowing seekers assert the
WE in unscreaming first STATE ‖ have buildings siege and surge
of zealotry ‖ und erstood.
the bearer of this notice practices THEOLOGY around but ACHING
with ABNORMALITY. we knows unknowingness.   the third
probability.

our LUNGS
our LUNGS, a lonesome
tin mechanism, the
water around

have this place NEGLIGABLE
GRIEF: mention the oceans we which
in these words of an embryo never
are in waking light, in demolition, in city

but rather EINER frustration: a beautiful statue worn
muttering through action // lustpended // one through muscle
one through question of lonesome

PATHOLOGY // a bleeding pantheon

a gift is the city and the setting of work
a gift of the foreherein Organism old also

these phantasms spin
around, they drive
absurd universes

in THEM
we is
      from US
PROGRESS
           (esparto seeded paper
an example of the CLASSIFICATION
           (rush of ex parte

be PLAY
      (and mute

they are out of habit ordinary
to wage a calm upstanding
WAR: spate of letters
(a WAD): Organization by MINT

a MYTH orients – see seven whole
vision on vision REALITY is GUILT
worn halos we is about NOUNs
aspect / idea

leaving PRIMITIVE happinesses
a PILL ist more NATURALe

a dark signer
see them unBEKNOWnst stammer
or wrecklesss SPIRITism
the good order sparring
we leaps // we weeps at these
spangles bout
cross into THEM, carry them TO

we is from thick PSYCHOLOG-I'ZED kultur

wreckage remembers that which
we is // that acreage // we ought
makes for MIGHT
we writes the NEW HISTORY
says THE BODY is one WE
is a PLAYFUL
(shining)   PLAYthing
apparatus of dys—

only soften it, the WATTAGE
so as to secure the eyes

to uplift the bellow set straight extreme
it is the gift that DIESEL
a SPEECHMAKING order
        (when under them
                (a heist

an order of is lonesome DISEASE // is halting night
set against the ONE stone chest of we
        a lost AUFGABE as seldom practiced
        tacit making :: the system an ideology
        BELIES the self selecting APPARATI

yet. each absight reducts the we
is come upon
PHYSIOLOGY
                rending // the hearing a viewing of
                the hearing a viewing

the Capital is here near the view of the organ
"it" – we is to inhale. all w/ in the thought
how we or us in which correct empire return

ENTER TALE:

guests of our NS answer UNSWER bewaringly
the middle of we all knows OCCUPATION
and consequences [THEY are PREMEDITATED
leaps made across the reel – the true sorrow

name and then

a righteous again from the right
assault sondaged organization here
while the HISTORY SPEAKS it
the response is getting educated

MAINTAIN |SECURE| BORDERs (criminal ASPECTS
spits. then leaves.
unRELENTING trauma is also PSYCHOLOGY
with all in HUNGER-war building war
WE is natural REALITY—we SICK
is I from REPUBLIK

under them a FLUSH the western
afforded NORMAL read before
in the interest
DIPLOMAT
        pre-selected over-WE
        in the interest of
DOW

out of EASE-grinding we unseen

heal LUNGS, leaden, a planned i's through KONFLIKT

we is the COMMON
material in DYNASTY

detained

the WALL a bare WAIT enters FAINT

diving, that dying   signs

i'sick

A PERSON IS MADE
patient

tracking is AMBIVALENT

another we is making words

berating

this, AN ACT OF PATRIOTISM, we writes it

[the bearer of this notice practices ABNORMALITY around
but aching with PSYCHOLOGY]

how WE & how place WE

                    as COUNTRY
                    at times of
                    & no person

how it is not
& how it is
WITH place

                                angling there

real time is real & not without

time unavowed and tightly stayed – grief
                           one tight PUNKTURE

there alone by posture an "I PLAYs
TONGUE," nothing but for SHINE
          (only salted for lick
so vile – the problem is where, a

grief otherwise another's, BODY OR
understanding of BODY, out and
forgotten   moss we takes on
awaiting
                    be atoned, that we thought only

the body or against the body
we has not another way

other world is always object world
          reality a bounce
                    (around 5
                    (around kinder period

so language that volley environing
with over-i's work is nothing for to lick
the festering one, all germaine be THEY
      (shining
      FORGIVENESS found not in FUTURE TENSE
a site when that is to BE
is not the NOW only
the STATE we's always in – only
                i's distracting
inspired PATTERN-SPEAKING is not the TO BE
but the IS
happens tremendous
dictated wresting of FAITH
      (shining
of we is TRUTH and LIGHT all ins

a compass eternal // the object

      (it burns

a refined bitter GARTEN // the literature we is

translating to AMERIKAN-fine upstanding YOU

that we   leaves you

a PRINCIPLE actuating agency

we is armed existence w/o WOR

the RAT klinging in the RAT HAUSE
is REGRESSIVisms
                (the much to question

                a sway
the program, it is when worked
            an APPARATUS

                (two fold sign
                    (a has been holds

hold tight acreages

answer's solution // answer's solution
tactik // diesel

a quelled // embittered // battlement befriending the gesture
kind wonder when under them   submit the shown BEAUTY
that we // [in it we all

a heist we

knows // leans against the LIED

stricken unjust a LONESOME hegemonic inherency
            the self through onLOOKER
            balances the VERIFIED
            scrapes the SHEET a triggered calculator
            all froms crooked HAS I HOLDS

and the PROJEKTion LIGHTS us
        (a sWAY hypnotic

all unknowingness cast
as MIGHT
over frightened NOW
as in it we alls

goes.   the stamen // comes out for morning
                    [functions of insult]

a *normal*–more *stable*   crescendo

nocturnal hazing

                                    of I is broader terms

                        so in it we all goes
how I and FORESIGHT | citizens

                    INHALES

                                    divine
(mining granite)   art of middle lung

                    remains
                    //
remains

[pretense]

then RISERS terminated reason
who saying unsure FAMILY, the case

lengthens itself – o, we knows KULTUR
not, very warlike this luck of SWINE

seen as DIESEL interrogations
REASON TERMINATED THROUGH YEAR

          (escalation a desirous

this sexuality is now a person (the rift
and know it felt so knowing of it
the OBJECT small words become
SPECTACLE w/o SPIEL
our lungs lonesome halt

soundn't spaken: INHALE.

a song from DUST
     (cold drill
leach upon the ghetto
wisening out of mouth

        money made that which
        the starker days
            (cultural significance
        sexualize the OBJECT

eye makes RIGHT
side-glance
        (ENVY
a ritualized. against der KULTUR

broken muscle AND RIGHT
where all langering furls from endorphins to WAR
a FOND ignorance we calls it
this that is sprung of METTLE
and lending spaces
      veterans MISPLACED limbs
      that trivial uttering
encamped unfolding
      surreptitious following

when we is HERE
in the ORGANized ORGANization
         that LEFT
is early sick that ROSE LIGHT

MYSTIK TRANCE AMERIKA

hidden stretchers elast the bending micro

war. what is seen–permitted / that's just torn
the tree and the work, or, a tree and a work

hear EVEN

           so in it we all goes how I

ROLL

           sullen who right for TASK

we straw characters we knows
surface. we INHALES untenable
celebration – we wise ART
besiege that HATE is is
RELIGION of ONE
casting a rending TIME
weighted not in swimming
on land. diesel burns

SILENCE now
all now here
having had

what is to carry we FORward

and the chalk
is the utterance. one can go far in
A WORD NOT WIDE SPOKED,

        a straight handle
        that total stammer:
        consequence
        don't make it milky sweet that is hand
        felt, not self. not that hot light. it is
        good, the leaving also of desire. even

ALONE is the OBJECT
        like out of grief when here
                there SUN – short
                sound storage lent

        when we is wise over LANGUE one
        may open a free hand but a machine
            tenable common
        wisdom we finds it
            so absurd all gender
        while the after is not left, the ethic.

a whisper is the spectacle of ache
is apparatus in this all worn libido
stricken fixer : obligate bleeder
begrieving that regal population

before nothing CONSTRUCT
inhales reservations we has PLACE
named for shining, absent soldiers
absent all saints – we is
aggression neutral

noways a word out of going
a person from a sight to be
it is then correct to empty lust
sick // broken with fear

the building a sin
of war among and escalation

one forgotten is one REMAINDERING
so saying LANGUE spake it faster
      most deliverABLE packAGE
insulation is free sick touching on all
endearments drink each to then a RINGER
FATHER // SHAFT // HISTORY
able speech against the leaving we
is what is left
of SOUNDAGED assembly
stricken solidarity

grief – is waiting
all the bodies arrange in three
dysfunction of thinking as a hearing
we listens and the first drift–dysphoric

mere puppet
silence equally divided is one
imperfect. terse. moan.
color collapsing – rising

INHALES
mind is two lines, or stands
a singing oracle
or a swinging oracle, able sung

real and under a flush: AWE
is also. was once. by midbreath

a rift between
all set scene

diesel builds the nests
born // RICH AND ARMED
in essential borders the SPRAWL
                    lucrative knowingness
gen up how very
how graded these
by right an open I has fuller

today mitigated tribe against the alone

wartime Amerikas
stands undreamt, which noon
often bars the traded hunger
duty the short quarter eros

greysome hateful prize
we holds zeal for western sutures
unsure laying across war time
even when the after is not leaving

standing; biding time around

WE is animal, darling. and water
go fuel this air walking
is it object manufactured
SCRIPTS OF SALT

the beginning word *ist infertile*
yes, out there well words do not fall
over the walkway says : CHIDED
be inclusion of word. the idea – ease

problems end, first one – how the one
mindsight will otherwise sicken all
seen. it must enter the LUNGS
though made of HAVE | HOLDS
so collapsed. wisen faint.
in water around the LUNGS: DIES.

//

OCCUPATION may not anesthetize
land. air. and sea. manning the STATE

still waged

when night is unassisted trench
color and sound be turned up
cards. WE is now to overcome
them ARMS. a stiller word biding

functions. as from sitting our TENDENS
CLASH. hungerSALT against the plate
of sorrow. diesel is burning ABJECT
institutions occupy PLACE. that RED

spatter dictates demolitions. figures
from neglect built-in. air eroticized
dissent antAGONIZING. WE is
ARMED FIGHTING AS A SCIENCE

ground structures sell the shaft, be
FUNDAMENT. be takers of SKY.

the tight history lending years
for arms; dies happily stricken
with SPEECH NATURE so very wide
lauded through PERSON rioting
the good negate the I by WE
SELF to arm, to arm, for calm
that alone reforms been had

        Apostle Critic
        amending
        masses. −names. −yr mothers.

        in kind
            let the assassinations commence

          war is einer TEXT
            overwrought end

WE is now to overcome you
a zealot deserving
biding a stiller word
a sea structure halt
a campaign *of culture*

from seated tendons
I is now to overcome YOU
object takers of sky
sites. and. hammers.

WE sells shaft
       most there

is nothing. searing bows
against PLACE the SORROW

we says
one would like DICTATIVE AUTHORITY
one would in the area of courts
rationale. tatter unbuilt principal
not wonder when under them drunk

desires leaden // the MENTION
some hearing GOD and SPRUCE through to Armageddon
a fledgling bereavement how yes aught dust

the just question the sorry the winning
winter ground drank overlying learnt
the one losing question
can all these wages spent
by a people yet to become

the BIOLOGY must then be WAKING
       Triebansprüche verstärkt
that i's question not of asked
       flew having restless (so viele
postures and DEVOUT
       endnommen
the inner world we knows anOTHER
waged from a wisening wills
the tacit / locked IDENTITY binding
business end // all's object identified

and out of giving—so through having had

the METHOD

[pretense]

we is deliberate
misdeeding we, the early
seeking Religion against the ONE
illusion far beyond ART

is able cunning
as is leaving
CONSTRUCT should be named
here

of people HUNGRY

WE understands.

in an even stead – all the dreamers disguised
EMPIRE SAPLINGS. UNrelative
s make their intellectual/intelligence function

[a quality RELATION] | enraged energy

> then we of OUR GUNS lay patient
> our OBLIGATION: people in this
> ALIVE
> object swimming HE | I | EINER

> another intuitive veiling of fatigues
> TEMPLE of war a lonesome disease

> [but w/ language] leavening interests the
> work

self-erotic forfeiture
> PARANoider SCRAPED SKY

the gentle is otherwise | an absence of ways

afterWORDs.

ACREAGE MAKES MIGHT // this, an act of PATRIOTism

this, an act of PATRIOTism, be MANIFEST
be DESTINY // etiology and incidence of
we // the BODY // tends
to hasten–cerebral metabolism
affect sudden change in ENVIRONMENT
we hasn't the palsy recognized w/ in-
creased PROGRESSion

obstruction // made limitless
expansion [IMAGE = not IDENTITY although held) as such]

in we the fast ENDEAVORING righting the
BAILING the
we the fast lending the fasting having been lent

in we aggressive // as a body // border
forces expel

beCAUSE JUDICIOUS care may result
in substantial improvement we makes RIGHT

DEMENTIA, place

caused by structural neuropathologic alterations
colonial sutures // THE HISTORY having been THE NEW having

                                                     now been

may give c(l)ue::

the NEW HISTORY calling we writes for THEM, having had all story adjusted as such, teach the peoples what they will KNOWS   by rote repeating // no disclaimer in time it wills be not   the NEW but THE. we, having drawn taut lines about the Mindfulness as such GROUP identity, do not escape the FUNDAMENTALS of who we   is, who we is made to be : : one   fiscal   determinant. THERE being ONE body we finds it   by extension, the true satisfaction ist   FINANCIAL IST   accountable to [berate the land // use destructivISMs // charge by sessions] ::   wreckage DISPENSE the factory forward-thinking sanctions dispute against THEY not we   calling all WINDs and CHIMEs tunnel beneath fanfare//pipeline eruption.   the shining frustration   that we is unsure contagion kultur   not building and in wider   white having fury and calling them   armed fighting with the WORD as conquest // as aSERVICE

the NATION, we the true calling   up to arms to arms for calm   a peace with SOLITARY RESISTANCES. speaks   the NEW HISTORY speaks it—   calls it a stammer // that

FREUDian situationISM

IN DEISEL politiking // we all goes as we goes

whom RIGHTthinking places ASPIRE transgressivISn'ts   of a peoples unspoken of a peoples WANTS of a peoples FREE REIGN